Colouring In

Colouring In

The Four Seasons of Four Poets

Amelia Fielden (Australia)
Gerry Jacobson (Australia)
Genie Nakano (USA)
Neal Whitman (USA)

Coordinated and edited by Amelia Fielden

Colouring In: The Four Seasons of Four Poets
ISBN 978 1 76041 099 5
Copyright © text individual poets 2016
Copyright © this collection Amelia Fielden 2016
Cover: Elaine Whitman and 'pling

First published 2016 by
GINNINDERRA PRESS
PO Box 3461 Port Adelaide SA Australia
www.ginninderrapress.com.au

Contents

Introduction: Sonja Arntzen		7
Spring		**11**
Bright New Leaves	Gerry Jacobson & Genie Nakano	13
'Hope Springs Eternal'	Amelia Fielden & Neal Whitman	17
Growing Wild	Amelia Fielden & Genie Nakano	22
Summer		**25**
Sunlight Between Dark Pools	Genie Nakano & Gerry Jacobson	27
'Of Cabbages and Kings'	Amelia Fielden & Neal Whitman	30
Unusual Shells	Genie Nakano & Amelia Fielden	34
Autumn		**37**
Planting Peace	Gerry Jacobson & Genie Nakano	39
'Season of Mist…'	Neal Whitman & Amelia Fielden	43
Fluttering Gold	Amelia Fielden & Genie Nakano	47
Winter		**49**
Burrowing Deep	Genie Nakano & Gerry Jacobson	51
Unicorns and Plum Blossoms	Neal Whitman & Amelia Fielden	55
The Perfect Canvas	Genie Nakano & Amelia Fielden	58
Acknowledgements		60
About the Poets		61

Introduction

The four seasons are embedded in the foundation of the Japanese poetic tradition. When Anglophone tanka poets organize collections of their poems, they often turn to the seasons for section categories just as Japanese poets have done for a millennium. Why are the seasons so compelling as both a source of poetic inspiration and an organising principle? Perhaps it is because tuning one's attention to seasonal turns makes one alive to change in all its manifestations. The realm of natural ephemera serves as a mirror for the ever-shifting mind.

This collection joins the tanka of two Australian poets and two American poets. Using the seasons as an organising principle in this work relativises the whole notion of seasons. The calendar months and cultural observances may be the same between the countries in the two hemispheres, but the seasons of sensual experience are reversed. In Australia, Christmas is observed with trips to the beach and BBQs. In America, December is the depth of winter, not the height of summer. An Australian poet can journey out of autumn a mere eighteen hours and arrive in spring in the northern hemisphere. Yet, spring is always spring no matter the name of the month it may occur in. This work encourages alacrity of mind in the reader. It allows one to skip round the globe without having to suffer jet lag.

My tangential involvement with this project began with an inquiry from Amelia Fielden about the colours associated traditionally with the four seasons in Japan. Spring was easy; spring is always green wherever it happens anywhere in the world. And red (for this volume, the shade of scarlet) was easy to designate for autumn because of the famous scarlet maple leaves of Japan and the many other kinds of trees round the world whose leaves turn red before they fall. Winter too is clearly white when one thinks of its characteristic manifestations in frost and snow. But summer, what about summer? There is no particular colour for summer in Japan; perhaps that is true for the rest of the world too. I suggested 'black' in reference to Sei Shōnagon's famous pronouncement:

> In summer, the night – moonlit nights, of course, but also at the dark of the moon, it's beautiful when fireflies are dancing everywhere in a hazy flight. And it's delightful too to see just one or two fly through the darkness, glowing softly. Rain falling on a summer night is also lovely. (*The Pillow Book*, translated by Meredith McKinney, Penguin Classics, 2006)

Nonetheless, I could understand why the idea did not fly. The back-up suggestion was purple for the wisteria of early summer. The first poem in the 'summer' section of the *Kokinshū*, the first and most revered of the imperial waka/tanka collections in Japan, takes wisteria as its topic:

> at my dwelling
> waves of wisteria are blooming
> just now on my pond!
> oh, mountain cuckoo when
> will you come and sing?

But waka on wisteria are actually few and far between, and I doubt that any Japanese person would immediately associate the colour purple with summer. And yet, as Genie Nakano's tanka in the summer section 'Unusual Shells' attests, it is fitting to have purple in the four season colour set, if only as a subtle nod to the great writer, Murasaki (literal meaning 'purple') author of the *Tale of Genji*, a work of poetry and fiction at the apex, the mature summer of the Japanese literary tradition.

This collection of tanka nods also to the Japanese poetic practice of linked verse, in which the two and three line segments of a waka/tanka are linked together to form a chain of verse. In this book, each tanka is independent and whole on its own, but each succeeding tanka is written in response to the one before. Although the section may start with seasonal imagery, the process of responding sometimes takes the sequence out of a seasonal mode. Amelia's search for unusual shells on a summer beach sparks in Genie the memory of a lost golden charm among perfume bottles. Or falling leaves can morph in the next tanka into a small dancing child. These sequences delight by moving in surprising directions and yet always providing resolution by returning to sound a seasonal tonic chord.

There is music in this volume, a silent music of orchestrated images as well as mellifluous sound wrought from simple language. The ingenious structure of the work and the pairing of poets of two hemispheres takes the 'old' of seasonal reference and makes it new.

Sonja Arntzen
Professor Emerita of Japanese Literature
University of Toronto

Spring

Green

Bright New Leaves   Gerry Jacobson & *Genie Nakano*

it's wet walking
along the Ridgeway
jumping
in clay puddles
as rain greens my face

playing in the rain
the rain plays with me –
opening my mouth
I taste the sky
seven flavours of rainbow

the little ones
take their bath together
flood the bathroom,
mummy is cross
weather is stormy

waiting
for the sun to shine
restless
here inside –
let's race up the highest hill

monkey's
up the mango tree
revelling
in her morning tea
wearing rainbow colours

ginger, cardamon
cinnamon, black tea 'n' milk
my morning chai
now I am ready
to greet the day

companion
of many caffeined
mornings
my leatherbound life
my loves…my longing

*I sing upon a star
coyote near my side
earth trembles
with aches and growing pains
of a birth long overdue*

boy baby
overflows with milk
regurgitates
over me…smiling,
his bottom burbles

*Ganesha statue
gives milk at the temple…
travelling
around the world
miracles revealed*

falling in love
with the power
and passion
of my own dance,
becoming Lord Shiva

your pose
looks unbalanced
ready
to topple over
a gentle breeze will do

breeze off the lake
touches my skin
standing
in Tree Pose, willows
with bright new leaves

together
we salute the morning sun
opening to life
touch the ground, rise again
as the sky fills with light

'Hope Springs Eternal'   Amelia Fielden & *Neal Whitman*

oh bluebells
spring after spring here
focused
on blossoms and daffodils
what else have I missed

'hope springs eternal'
gardeners are optimists
wish lists in winter…
today at the nursery
we run into old friends

the wildest
friend in my school years
now cultivates
sedate behaviour
in her granddaughters

when green blades rise
Pacific Grove celebrates
the good old days
in the park clowns, jugglers
dogs and children off leash

'He is risen
… He is risen indeed'
the response
never doubted in childhood
the belief long vanished

like Athena
sprung from the brow of Zeus
something new
takes root in our household
seven thousand steps a day

here we go
round the lake again
fresh willow fronds
stroke the rippling waters ---
some grey on her muzzle now

seal pup season
brings families to the shore
oohing and aahing
young ones will not remember
they too once mewled and suckled

the whiteness
of lambs and daisies
dotted through fields,
of baby bottles with milk
for feeding the orphans

as we sailed out
optimism prevailed
on opening day
no salmon to be found ---
faith is broad, doubt is deep

sun glinting
on aquamarine
waves warm enough
to swim without a wetsuit
weightless meditation

nothing amiss
the surface appears calm
WHOOSH
a gap opens…rip tide
time to renew marriage vows

before bedtime
we need to walk our dogs
watching the path
not the moon and the stars –
romance wanes, love remains

dropping sun
'L'heure bleue' turns to 'noir'
in the twilight
Venus gives rise to desire
one shared cup of honey wine

Growing Wild   Amelia Fielden & *Genie Nakano*

>   market stalls
>   displaying tulips –
>   can it be
>   a year since I was here
>   choosing the brightest bunch

> *daffodils*
> *everywhere, growing wild*
> *we took photos*
> *a daffodil in my hair*
> *one behind your ear*

>   near the lake
>   still chilly to the touch
>   greening grass
>   speckled with dandelions
>   where the picnic rug is spread

> *dandelion wine*
> *'packing all the joys of summer*
> *into a single bottle…'*
> *let's drink it this Sunday*
> *celebrating with every sip*

I've stayed away
too long remembering
our differences
forgetting the fun,
the many things we shared

your spicy
might still be too bland
for me –
trying not to criticize
we seek a balanced blend

a new season
time to spring into action
the evenings
are growing milder,
not so my passion

mockingbird
all night I listen
to your sweet songs
knowing what you want,
knowing what I want

chocolate eggs
from the Easter Bunny
'peace and goodwill
you're welcome as the flowers
on Mockingbird Hill'

Summer

Purple

Sunlight Between Dark Pools   Genie Nakano & *Gerry Jacobson*

ice cream melts
on chubby fingers
in July
city centre about to fry
the siren blasts a tragedy

after our swim
we three children sit
with cold drinks,
wishing this would
last forever…

Dad floats
Mum teaches me
swimming
I was one with water
before I could walk

the Teign river
ripples and sparkles
in sunlight
between dark pools ---
so does my life

my lover says
a childhood of hardship
made me strong ---
perhaps it's brought us together
moving into the light

Bogong moth
fluttering on the floor
beside me…
we move together
when the music starts

quite a plain girl
wearing muted colours…
they dance all night
as I watch them, wondering
what's she got that I haven't

moody
January noon
sultry
sleepy…languid
with summer love

off the wall
into a mid-summer night
with firefly sky
crickets in competition ---
pinch me…is this real

Christmas morning
cicadas chirping
flies buzzing
mosquitos biting
cockatoos squawking

you're hot, I'm cold
on the other side of the world
I imagine you
to be here with me, blazing
while my heart is on fire

'Of Cabbages…and Kings' Amelia Fielden & *Neal Whitman*

December
first summer month downunder –
a freckled kid
climbs on sweaty Santa's knee
wishing for a surfboard

July
pool parties and rock 'n' roll
then slow dancing
our teen bodies clinging,
hormones in overdrive

feasting over
Christmas night is beach walks
watermelon
family chats and plans
for the long vacation

an OPEN flag
waves over the snack shop,
fish 'n' chips
draw gulls to my beach bench –
how little they know me

January glare
bouncing off the deep blue sea,
sand sticking
to my hot, sunscreened skin
ah, the cold shower feels good

a short shower
then sun floods the fairway
I play the back nine
like water off a duck's back
eight pars and one birdie

night tennis
under floodlights I find
my first lover
a holiday romance
ends in lifelong friendship

sunset sail
across Half Moon Bay
sipping white wine
we make two friends our age
like us, they do not text

chill the glasses
let's slip another shrimp
on the barbie
and bluetooth the Beatles ---
oldies are goldies

closing up
our divine rental cottage
we speak not
of cabbages…and Kings
but of emails and deadlines

so brightly green
leaves on the maple trees
and watered lawns
in the March suburbs
nowhere yet brown or scarlet

like fanning
a ringed book of paint swatches
adjacent squares
not different in colour, but
a shift in tone – summer's end

Unusual Shells Genie Nakano & *Amelia Fielden*

melons
bursting on the vine
dripping
with sweetness, our eyes
clung to each other

summer evenings
lingering on the deck
in a soft haze
we sipped chilled moscato
deferred our sleeping time

war still rages,
deployed you leave tomorrow
intoxicating
Lady of the Night flowers
…gone by sunrise

at low tide
I wander the warm sands
searching
for unusual shells
to show you, whenever

I've found
amongst old perfume bottles
a small gold charm
you had left hidden,
almost lost to me

*the fragrance
from wisteria in bloom
round my window
drifts through my dreaming
with lavender and lilac*

purple:
majestic mountain peaks,
Murasaki
and her Tale of Genji,
royal colour through the ages

*relentlessly
crickets thrum in the garden
these short hot nights
I think of you awake
at your foreign post*

in the darkness
I imagine the dangers
of the desert –
missing you, missing us
let's ride the summer wind

Autumn

Scarlet

Planting Peace   Gerry Jacobson & *Genie Nakano*

scuffling
golden brown leaves,
strolling
through light grey rain,
inside – I'm dancing

falling leaves
whirling dervishes
spin
spiral upwards
to another entity

the little one
ventures the dance floor
twirling
into her future
I whirl in what's past

music in the room
gets us rocking on our feet
we turn around
lose our heads
fall in love again

falling
for that dancing girl
all painted up
on the wall of a cave
for twenty thousand years

cold and dark
the warmth of summer gone
that dream again…
I ride a Camargue horse
bareback across the marshlands

walking the dyke,
kissed by raindrops
striding ahead
smelling the sea…
end of a journey

he wants out
I think we should go on,
times are rough
rivers must keep flowing —
how deep is the ocean

gliding slowly
through a narrow channel
steering
between two rocky islands
one's his…and one's hers

crash, bling, blink
china across the room, then
she's out the door —
old patterns need to change,
talking is not enough

blessed are those
who plant peace
this season —
they shall harvest
and eat in the spring

'Season of Mists and Mellow Fruitfulness' Neal Whitman & *Amelia Fielden*

fall…
its scent suggests what was lost
forbidden fruit
to autumn: I lift my hat
and toss it in the wind

words blown about
by the April breezes
colouring
my tanka in shades
of crimson and gold

for the leaf of me
oops…I mean the life of me
what could be better
than to promenade
beneath Japanese maples

brocaded hills
above brown rice paddies
November
travelling through the valleys
of Honshu Island

was it fall
Adam and Eve left Eden?
how they must have missed
their quilted meadowland,
its glorious fabric

apples
the rosy sheen of their skins
sweet, juicy
the crunchy whiteness
of their flesh – oh, Delicious

whipped cream
topping my Irish coffee
topping pumpkin pie
what can surpass these riches?
a second helping, please

*a pumpkin each
to make jack o'lanterns
at Halloween
I can never celebrate
with far off grandchildren*

Canada geese
in vee formation honking
at dusk
when temperatures drop
our house guests too head south

over the lake
sunsets ever more brilliant
these days
of 'declining sun' –
an old man gazes westward

winter's discontent
spring, the mud season
summer doldrums –
as for me, I profess
to being an autumn amorist

persimmon globes
glowing from bare branches
against blue sky…
can any season
rival this in beauty

Fluttering Gold   Amelia Fielden & *Genie Nakano*

Zen garden
crammed with solemn tourists
photographing
the first few scarlet leaves
on a small maple tree

October
leaves crunching under my feet
the bite
of a first red apple…
the day you died

across the world
spring flowers in bloom
Halloween
kids tricking or treating
on a bright warm night

oh, the wind
the wind is what sets us free
on a dark autumn night
spirits fill the air
swirled with van Gogh stars

sunflowers
ablaze in their frame
at the Gallery
and in my memory
of past summers' hot fields

all the poems
we wrote together
memorized,
we're here now to sing them
as gingkos flutter gold

Winter

White

Burrowing Deep Genie Nakano & *Gerry Jacobson*

Governor declares
our city is in drought –
barefoot
in the falling rain
happy I don't believe

oh there's
carbon in the air
and the levee is dry
for the climate
is a changin'

sky don't cry!
trees looking up to you
are dying
from your tears
that drop as acid rain

*ribbon gum next door
attacked by chainsaws –
I leave the house
to dull the pain
with tea and cake and poetry*

prose
keeps the insane, sane –
after I'm underground
I'll have no use for words
earth churns winter into spring

*out of tombs
and sepulchres
the wildwood grows
fertilised
by forgotten griefs*

seeds
blown to foreign lands
burrowing deep
into black lava sands
a hybrid survives

Australian airman
'neath English turf
Since
1941
'greater love hath no man'

pulling me down
the cries of living ghosts –
mankind
with war and bombs
sets the earth on fire

scarred
by broken glass
my playground
rubble and ruin
the bomb sites of London

ashes, ashes
fallen on snow
the mulberry tree
blooms again –
nature changes, never dies

crunching frost
in the glow of dawn
and the full moon
hanging out up there
with Jupiter and Venus

Unicorns and Plum Blossoms Neal Whitman & *Amelia Fielden*

fall is defunct
emails a Russian relative ---
where I live
her crevice of dawn
portends short, dark days

long evenings
of comfort food and reading
in winter
we met, courted in spring
married in summer

what's for dessert?
bread and butter pudding
by the fireside
my poodle and I
eyeball each other

some mornings
there's a dankness of fog...
more often
her tiny paws patter
over silvery frost

this month's *Vogue*
declares the new black to be
black and white –
now in fashion, magpies
strutting down our driveway

cosy in bed
in my childhood home
I worried
and wondered where birds slept
when tree limbs iced over

when young I
welcomed snowploughs at night
School's Cancelled –
today I dig out the car
dreading a tough commute

four together
in a ski gondola
up the mountain…
all those years wondering
whether she'd have children

snowy owls
sighted in the canyon
how people flock
to see white animals
wolves, whales, and unicorns

plum blossoms
in the last month of winter
Tokyo-ites
gather to appreciate
these harbingers of spring

The Perfect Canvas   Genie Nakano & *Amelia Fielden*

sunshine sails
through unclouded blue
no snow on board –
my wounds have healed
leaving no scars behind

what's not there
to like about a day
when the ice
is melting from the front steps
as we set out hand in hand

no more secrets
take off those woollen gloves,
skin to skin
let's stroll around the lake
where plum trees are in bud

pushing through
the dark winter months
crocuses
white purple yellow
beneath leafless elms

black branches
framing an empty sky,
the perfect canvas
for whatever
one wants to become

Acknowledgements

Fluttering Gold (Amelia Fielden & Genie Nakano) was previously published in *Skylark, A Tanka Journal* 3:1, Summer 2015, edited by Claire Everett

Unusual Shells (Genie Nakano & Amelia Fielden) was previously published in *Kokako* 22, 2015, edited by Patricia Prime & Margaret Beverland

About the Poets

Born in Sydney, Australia, **Amelia Fielden** has lived in Japan, England, Morocco and Malta, and has also spent substantial periods of time on the west coast of North America. Amelia is a professional translator, and an enthusiastic writer of traditional tanka-style poetry in English. She has had published twenty-three translations of Japanese literature, seven collections of her own poetry, and four collaborative books. In addition, Amelia has also edited, or co-edited, six other themed anthologies of English language tanka.

Gerry Jacobson lives in Canberra, Australia's capital. In a past life, he worked as a geologist. Now he travels to visit grandchildren in Sydney and Stockholm, writing tanka in the cafés of those cities. Gerry also composes 'tanka prose', which has been published in journals including *Haibun Today* and *Atlas Poetica*. His recent chapbook, *Dancing with Another Me*, celebrates his resurrection as a dancer.

Genie Nakano was born in East Lost Angeles, California. She holds a Masters in Dance from UCLA. An award-winning writer of non-fiction, Genie is also a poet/columnist for *Rafu Shimpo* and the *Gardena Valley News*. She is the author of two poetry books, *Enter the Stream* and *Storyteller*, and a yoga manual. Genie experiments with music, dance, and theatre in her tanka performances. Some of her performances can be found on Genie Nakano, Youtube channel.

On the path to **Neal and Elaine Whitman**'s front door is a stone slate incised in Latin: 'from the east light/from the west fruit'. Indeed, both were born on the east coast of USA and are now retired on its west coast. Neal's award-winning poetry still spans the North American continent, as he is a member of the New England Poetry Club and the San Francisco Bay Area Poets' Coalition, as well as the Tanka Society of America.

www.ingramcontent.com/pod-product-compliance
Lightning Source LLC
Chambersburg PA
CBHW070051120526
44589CB00034B/1909